ALL THAT LIVES

VALERIE LAWS

Red Squirrel Press

First published in the UK in 2011 by
Red Squirrel Press
Holy Jesus Hospital
City Road
Newcastle upon Tyne
United Kingdom
NE1 2AS
www.redsquirrelpress.com

Red Squirrel Press is represented by Inpress Ltd.
www.inpressbooks.co.uk

Cover image: Axial ^{99m}Tc-Exametazime SPECT
scan of brain with advanced Alzheimer's.
Image supplied courtesy of Sean J. Colloby and
John T. O'Brien.

Cover and text design: Andrew Edwards

A CIP catalogue record is available from the British Library
ISBN: 978-1-906700-43-0

Printed by Martins the Printers
Sea View Works
Spittal
Berwick-upon-Tweed
United Kingdom
TD15 1RS

ACKNOWLEDGEMENTS AND THANKS

The following poems won awards, and/or were previously published in books, magazines, anthologies, or online:
Lifting the Lid won a Commended Prize in the 2009 National Poetry Competition.
Benign and *In the Dissecting Room* won Commended Prizes in the 2010 Hippocrates Competition, *Stroking the Brain* ditto in 2011.
A Litter of Moons won 2nd Prize in the 2008 Mslexia Poetry Competition.
Sirenomelia won a Commended Prize in the 2009 Plough Competition, and was published online in *Ink, Sweat and Tears*.
Your skin will outlive you is published in *On Grand Central Station We Sat Down and Wept*, anthology ed.Kevin Cadwallender, Red Squirrel Press 2011.
Ghazal to my Lover and *Fighting Fire* were published in *Tadeeb International Quarterly*.

A major Wellcome Trust Arts Award (2008-9, with fellow *This Fatal Subject* project creator, artist Susan Aldworth) funded a residency at Gordon Museum of Pathology, King's College, London with access to KCL's medical school, scientists, and dissections, facilitated by Professor Susan Standring and William Edwards, Keeper of the Gordon. Heartfelt thanks to them both.
This Fatal Subject, culminating exhibition at Old Operating Theatre Museum, London, Jan-Feb 2009, featuring poems from the collection, was a *Guardian Guide Pick of the Week*.

At an early stage, the collection in progress won a Northern Writer's 'Time to Write' Award from New Writing North.

Newcastle University's Institute for Ageing and Health (IAH) funded my current residency (2010-11) through *Changing Age*, giving me access to many research scientists. My thanks to IAH Director Professor Tom Kirkwood for facilitating, Graham Armitage and Dr Lynne Corner for support.
My installation, *Slicing the Brain*, a sequence of dwindling versions of *The Incredible Shrinking Brain,* (reflecting the process of

dementia), *Slices of Brain, Senior Last Moments, In the Dissecting Room* (using screened animated text and recorded sound) formed part of a major exhibition, *Coming of Age*, with work by Degas, Renoir, Henry Moore et al at Great North Museum, Newcastle, January-March 2011. *Slices of Brain* is published in the catalogue for *Coming of Age*, 2011. Thanks to Lucy Jenkins, Curator.

Wellcome Trust also funded my 2009 residency for Darwin 200, *Evolving Words,* as Newcastle Poet Mentor, with access to scientists at the Sanger Institute, Cambridge, and Centre for Life, Newcastle. My thanks to Elizabeth Lynch, project director.

Thanks are due to those above, and to other scientists who gave so generously of their time and taught me so much; especially those below, in Newcastle and London, whose ground-breaking research directly informs these poems.

At IAH, Newcastle University: Professor Elaine Perry (neurochemical pathologist, collaborator on NDEs and consciousness); Professor Robert Perry (neuropathologist); Sean Colloby and Michael Firbank (SPECT and MRI scans, cover image); and former IAH Director, Professor Jim Edwardson.
At Institute of Neuroscience, Newcastle University: Professor Anya Hurlbert, Director of ION; Dr Fiona Lebeau (rat brains and waves); Dr Evelyne Sernagor (eyes).
Also Nigel Cooper, Home Office Pathologist, RVI, Newcastle upon Tyne.
At Kings College London, Professor Anthony Strong (strokes, neurone death).
At Guys, London: Professor Anthony Graham (embryologist).

El Gouna: the collection was pulled together during my residency at El Gouna, Egypt, in 2010. Thanks to Orascom, the Advisory Board, and to Bernardine Evaristo and Fadia Faqir for related support and other helpful offices.

'All that lives must die' William Shakespeare (*Hamlet*)

CONTENTS

7   ALL THAT LIVES Poems of dating and dying
8   DEDICATION
9   My Mother's Twin Lovers
10   Sharp Knives
11   Losing It
12   The Groucho Marx Guide to Dating
13   The Incredible Shrinking Brain I
14   The Incredible Shrinking Brain II
15   The Incredible Shrinking Brain III
16   The Incredible Shrinking Brain IV
17   The Incredible Shrinking Brain V
18   The Incredible Shrinking Brain VI
19   The Incredible Shrinking Brain VII
20   Senior Last Moments
22   Flirting at the Funeral
23   Telling My Mother's Heart To Stop
24   The Physics of Closed Eyes
25   Your Skin Will Outlive You
26   He runs ten miles to my house
27   Sex Tech
28   Pumping Ions
29   Circle of Willis
30   Aneurysm Umbrella
31   Stroking the Brain
32   Lifting the Lid
33   Last Call
34   Ghazal to my lover
35   THIS FATAL SUBJECT
36   A Litter of Moons
38   Sirenomelia Baby
39   From Fin to Fingers
40   'Girl has second head removed'
42   Cyclops Baby

43   Benign
44   Sausages After Amputation
45   In the Dissecting Room
46   Dissection Suite: Ten Oblique Views
49   'Indefinite Retention'
50   Slices of Brain
52   Rat Brain
54   Face Rat
55   Handyman
56   Fighting Fire
57   POEMS OF EVOLUTION AND AFRICA
58   In the Beginning was the Bang
59   Crunching the Numbers
60   Sonic the Hedgehog Killed Your Baby
61   Dark Matters
62   Walking back to Africa
63   Coming to Egypt to Write About Death
64   On Being Sexually Aroused by the Cheviot Hills

ALL THAT LIVES

Poems of dating and dying

DEDICATION

With love to my mother, Sheila, who died of Alzheimer's Disease, April 2005: and to my father, Lindsay, who died suddenly of an Aortic Aneurysm, March 2006.

Witnessing their deaths drove me to discover the science of dying down to cellular level, to celebrate the terrible beauty of the process and tell the story of the body's final journey.

MY MOTHER'S TWIN LOVERS

'I must get back to the men,' my mother announces,
Then slyly meets my eye, as I choose, this time,
To avoid my usual reply. 'I know what you're thinking!'
She's triumphant. 'That there's only one of them! But
You're wrong, you know!' My mother is having an affair.
She's cheating on my father with another man, who lives
With them, looks like his twin, and even shares his name.
'I think they must be cousins,' she explains, defiantly.

Before going to bed with my father, she slips next door,
Turns back the spare bed quilt, and leaves her slippers there,
So the other man won't suspect. She has doubled her marriage,
Two-timed adultery. After blameless years of barely moderation,
Let alone excess in anything, she now has a surplus of husbands.
It's as if in creating my father's double, she's conjured up her own
Wicked twin, denied a life 'til now, when time is running short.

She has gained an extra husband, while the one I had is gone,
Which is fine, but now my elderly mother, with dementia,
Has a more exciting sex life than I do, kicking up her heels
While mine have been dragging. Perhaps it's time, I think,
As I take her home to her lovers, for me to get back to the men.

SHARP KNIVES

My mother made me fearless of sharp knives.
At home, no 'always cut away from you'.
In her kitchen, we welcomed the blade,
Stroking a hand-held carrot's thick shaft
With skin-deep skill. I'd watch the knife
Approach, slicing through cellulose like a shark
Through shallows, dividing the crisp cells,
The glint of it emerge to stop
At palm or thumb-ball, denting my skin
As if testing a melon for ripeness;
Painless, bloodless. I can peel and chop
In my hand, knowing the knife I use
Like I know my own width through doors,
Like my mother knew her favourite knife
For cutting chips.

Some knives are too sharp to feel, too thin
To dent giving skin. My mother does not feel
The blade slicing into her brain, paring
Away her memories, cutting off the cells
Which hold her self, painless, bloodless.
Like the magician's assistant, she smiles
As the honed edge bites, dividing her from us
And from her history. Her knife-hardened hands
Can't feel their own idleness; she does not know
That she has forgotten how to use a knife
Even for cutting chips.

LOSING IT

Afternoon in the Day Centre, where
My mother 'looks after old folk', never
Tries to leave; but today, she quietly
Gets up, walks out unnoticed, emerging
Just as my father drives past on a random
Errand. Their eyes meet. Strange, he thinks,
Early finish? They should have said.
He stops. She gets into the car.

Coincidence? Black holes bubble
Her hippocampus, memories popping
Like fairy liquid foam: vacuolation.
Later, I see it on SPECT scans, brain slices
Like Halloween pumpkin faces, with
Drooping eye and mouth holes melting,
Blue, red, yellow flames, gaps in the brain
Growing as dementia digs its tunnels. But
Could there be wormholes, new connections
Forming, perhaps only for a second,
In that strange multiverse?

They are drinking G and T (Gordons,
Schweppes, lemon slices pre-frozen)
In their garden, not hearing the phone,
As the staff and I search the streets
For her, losing our minds.

THE GROUCHO MARX GUIDE TO DATING
('I don't want to belong to any club that will accept me as a member')

He's got a beer belly, his aftershave's smelly,
And just look at that sweater, I deserve something better!
There's no-one I'd date here, no way. Hold on, wait,

He's young, and he's pretty, he's fun and he's witty,
He's not a bit stout, and he's asking me out!
I carefully inspect him, I fully expect him
To turn out to be joking – he's so hot he's smoking!

But

I'm old and I'm crippled, I'm battered and wrinkled,
I'm deformed and I'm scarred, I've got two ingrown hairs,
I'm uneven and marred and have trouble with stairs,
I'm a husk, I'm a rind, I'm half out of my mind,
I'm awkward and stroppy, he's fit as a lop, he
Must be insane if he wants to date me.

That's it! He's flaky,
A psycho, a stalker, he's after my daughter,
Or after my money. No, on your bike honey,
If you're hitting on me, there's a flaw I can't see.
I can't be with a man, if he wants to be with me.

Obviously.

THE INCREDIBLE SHRINKING BRAIN I
(*a sequence of seven, reflecting the progress and effects of Alzheimer's disease*)

Excited, she tugs me up to her bedroom of thirty years.
'Look! There's all this here!' A sweep of her arm presents
Melamine wardrobes with fancy handles, the swagged
Pink curtains she sewed herself. Back downstairs,
'Look!' The hall: plates painted at an evening class
She took to keep her brain alert, ranged on the delft rack.
'See? It's all gone! But look!' Upstairs again,
A miracle – her bedroom's reappeared, like
An MFI-bought Brigadoon. The universe in her skull
Is shrinking, big crunching; and true to the predictions
Of physicists, her time is running backwards, rewinding
What she knows and understands. Something she learned
Playing peep-bo with her twin in the scullery kitchen
Is about to vanish, but she holds it for a moment,
Poised between knowing and not knowing.

She's amazed, her bedroom might still exist when
Out of sight; soon, she will unlearn this too. But today,
As her time runs backwards to a singularity, it feels to her
Like discovery, and today, I try to share her joy.

THE INCREDIBLE SHRINKING BRAIN II

                              her bedroom of thirty years
                         A sweep of
Melamine wardrobes   ,the swagged
Pink curtains she sewed herself.
         The hall: plates painted
             to keep her brain alert
             all gone
             – her

                              universe
Is shrinking,
              her time is running backwards, rewinding
What she knows and understands.
Playing peep-bo with her twin in the scullery kitchen
Is about to vanish, but she holds it
Poised between knowing and not knowing.

She   might still exist
Out of sight   she will unlearn.   But today,
her time runs backwards   her
                    discovery   her
joy.

THE INCREDIBLE SHRINKING BRAIN III

                        her   years
                      weep
A   war   ,
      she wed
    he   late
          her brain
   all gone
  – her
                      universe
shrinking,

Playing peep-bo with her twin in the scullery
  about to vanish,   she
    between knowing and not knowing.

She   might still exist

her time

                           her joy.

her   years

,

her brain
all gone
– her
universe
shrinking,

about to vanish   she
not knowing.

She   might still exist

joy.

her brain

all gone

– her

universe

she

not knowing.

She   is

joy.

                     her brain
            all gone
         – her

                         wing

                                      joy

THE INCREDIBLE SHRINKING BRAIN VII

gone

SENIOR LAST MOMENTS

You forget what it was you went upstairs for
You forget your glasses are on your head
You forget that it's shuffle, not raffle, the cards
You forget to notice you've made a mistake.

You sometimes forget who the man in your house is,
Or that you've been married for forty five years.
You forget that the old man in bed beside you, is
The young dashing airman who 'just left the room'.
You forget that your parents died decades ago,
And won't tell you off for getting home late.
Every night, you forget this, and fight to get back there,
Screaming and scared as an abducted child.

You forget 'son' and 'daughter', their names, but not faces,
You remember you love them - whoever they are,
You remember to laugh, and make jokes, and be playful.
You forget that you've walked til your ankle is broken,
You forget you're in pain and remember each minute,
Forgetting why.

You forget your manners, make comments, spit food out,
You forget how to eat with a knife, fork and spoon.
You don't hide the symptoms of your constipation
As your body forgets how to shift its own waste.
You forget to keep private your urination,
You forget the existence of shame and good taste.
You still eat, but your brain forgot how to use food,
You're starving, big bellied, on three meals a day.
You forget how to speak, you forget how to chew,
You forget how to swallow, as thirst forgets you.

Your brain's shutting down, beleaguered, defeated,
You can sit where you're put and you know how to smile,
Til you forget how to see, or move, or respond,
Your brainstem's on auto, the dinosaur relic,

That keeps your heart beating, your lungs breathing air,
And where now are *you*, do you hear, are you in there,
Do you know they are crying, and holding your hands?
Are you seeing your dead father come smiling to meet you
Or do you know nothing of your heart's last stand?

And now we remember we've almost forgotten
The you that we knew, who began to forget.

FLIRTING AT THE FUNERAL

A funeral for a friend. It was cold
That day, raining, damp in the church
Where a ship hung from the rafters,
Becalmed like me, embalmed and frozen.
I thought of the one who died, as I do still,
And of the younger man behind me, the night
We were suddenly kissing in his rain-wet car,
And he said, 'You're fucking gorgeous,'
And as if my dad or husband might appear
I scuttled in alone, and shut the door.

Now we crowded outside, leaving
Our friend to the fire. At the smoky bar
Our chilled hands touched. Jack Daniels,
Oily and amber, ignited my belly and breath,
Burning off long years of marriage. My head
Swam, drunk with lust, as around us mourners
Stared, and I didn't care, too full of joy, sadness,
Desire and Jacky D, his hand hot on my thigh,
His thumb already sliding under my skirt.

TELLING MY MOTHER'S HEART TO STOP
('Death is a process, not an event,' *Simpson's Forensic Medicine*).

I said to my mother's heart, stop
Please stop. I said it when my father left
The room, weeping. Cups of tea, Co-op
Sandwiches, the toilet, divided up our days,
While her heroic heart kept up its pointless beat,
Knocking against my ear from beneath the beams
Of her ribs, as her stubborn breathing rocked me,
Fuelling her tangled brain which could not answer.

But death is a process, not an event, and first,
There is somatic death, the body no longer
Able to reach out, or respond. Stop, please stop,
I told her heart when we were alone, no-one
Is coming to put things right, give in, spare
Yourself this unbearable, long labour,
Pushing drying blood round a dying body:
But it went on, and on. On the third day, parched,
Still punching sluggishly, it retreated to its core,
Purpling her bone-white limbs with silting blood.

For first there is somatic death, when heart and lungs
Stop, and so they did, slowing, resting between
Beats and breaths, longer and longer, until
There were no more. And then her cells began to die,
Few by few, like streetlights going out, for first
There is somatic death, and then there is cellular
Death, and death is a process, not an event.

THE PHYSICS OF CLOSED EYES

Closing your lids takes effort.
They don't drop like shutters,
Obedient to gravity like
The rest of your skin. Sleeping,
Your will keeps your eyes covered,
Safe from the light. I know this
Because I watched her eyes
Half-open, blind, for days,
As her body fought to live
And the water left her skin
As it left Mars, as it does
Before life leaves. Until
The end: when heart and lungs
Began to stop, they sprang
Wide open, the iris juicy
As a cat's, the pupils tiny
Black holes into which light fell
And died, taking my face with it.
I closed them for her, a fingertip
Holding down each lid, sealing in
Her last unseen sight of me.

YOUR SKIN WILL OUTLIVE YOU

'anticipating the heaven of actual touch,' Elizabeth Smart.

Do you know that your skin will outlive you?

My mother's, before they made me
Leave her, smelled so good against my face,
Like a baby's, purged of all impurity through her
Long dying: I didn't know then, it was still alive.

Whether the brain, like hers, dies first, killing
The breath, and with it, the heart: or like my father's,
Holds out until the struggling, suddenly blood-starved
Heart gives up, strangling brain, then breath:
Either way, the rest follow, bowels, liver, kidneys,

Until there's just skin, holding things together
In its quiet way for a day or two more, mute
Witness of our premature grief, the attendant's
Wash cloth, the clutching hands of the bereaved.

No-one told her skin it was time to be dead.
When I let her go for the last time, maybe
It registered, somehow, my hand on her arm.
Left alone, perhaps it was still
Anticipating the heaven of actual touch.

HE RUNS TEN MILES TO MY HOUSE

I'm at a garden party, on an English summer lawn,
Twirling my sunglasses while talking herbaceous borders,
When my lover texts me. 'R u in? I will run
2 yr house.' I tap out the code that sets him in motion,
And sit tight a spell, knowing as I discuss this hot weather
We're having, ten miles away he is running, running
To me, and it's me that's sweating, getting hot
Right through, my heart keeping time with the great
Engine of his marathon heart, driving the powerful pistons
Of his long arms and legs, the pounding of his feet,
His face grave, remote as if meditating. He is the biggest
Person I have ever seen close up, almost blue-black,
He is so not-me, that if we were birds, we'd be labelled
As different species. Sun scorches the grass to savannah
As I sip white wine, remembering him on stage with spear
And full regalia, the lion skin firing his courage
To sing his family's songs in a ten-mile voice. A massive
Presence, no less exotic now in lycra, he's devouring the miles
Between us, younger, athletic, beautiful, our brief summer a gift
Unlooked for. He's coming closer to the sun-yellow walls
Of my bedroom, the sun-bleached white of my sheets,
And I get up, 'I must be going', speed dialling a taxi home.

SEX TECH

I love the new technology of sex
And dating. The thrill of a booty text,
Or exchanging dirty talk over mobile phones,
And let me count the ways to be alone
I buy at the sex shop for women, so discreet,
Who cares that our window-cleaner's there, to greet
Me cheerily as I go in... Condoms, latex-free,
I get from Sainsbury's, where my father buys his tea,
And materialises just as I reach for them, so what,
I love it all, even buying AA batteries gets me hot.

To hell with twice-daily love letters, typed
Or scrawled, I've burned them all, I'd rather skype
And see my lover, everything I'm missing
On webcam when we can't be kissing.
Email double entendres, facebook updating,
While I was married all this was out there waiting,
A brave new world, for me to explore, embrace –
Are friends electric? Hell, yes!

PUMPING IONS

Inside my father's brain,
Like a stinging cell in a jellyfish
Each neurone is winding
Itself like a watch, tightening
Its spring, squeezing its skin, pumping
Sodium out, potassium in,

Defying the current in the fluid
It swims in, which would leach
Potassium out, leak sodium in.

High on sugar, prepared to lash out,
Crack its spark of a whip,
When a message arrives like a scent
In the wind, to fire! pass it on,
In a flash of relief, a flood of release,
Sodium in, potassium out.

On a chemical wave Nat King Cole,
Apple tart, trigger one then another
In a firecracker chain, but always renewed
Like magic candles which keep on igniting
While the neurone's rewinding,
Plumping and tightening,
Sodium out,
Potassium in.

THE CIRCLE OF WILLIS
A Villanelle

A spring welling up to the mind's castle keep,
The arteries rise with their blessing of blood,
Through the Circle of Willis, a crown buried deep.

At the base of the brain, out of injury's reach,
The vessels are linked, an arterial loop,
Both a fence and a well for the mind's castle keep.

If one artery's dammed, a drought-dried creek,
Or bursts through its banks in a salt red flood,
The Circle of Willis, a crown buried deep

Can allow for another to make up for the leak,
To let the brain breathe, to quickly make good
The supply of hot life for the mind. It may keep

The brain thinking, alive and complete,
As the royal physician first understood,
Thomas Willis, unearthing the crown buried deep.

Willis had his own circle, Wren, Locke, the elite
In the mid-sixteen hundreds, great minds who would
Begin to draw maps of the brain's castle keep:

But nothing is failsafe, nothing can keep
Even a King's brain from dying: nor could
Charles' Circle of Willis, with the axe buried deep.

Both a well and a wall for the mind's castle keep,
Built by time, sex, and chance: a ring of bright blood,
Salvation or stopgap. At a stroke, staunch or breached,
The Circle of Willis, our crown buried deep.

ANEURYSM UMBRELLA

Hooked on the heart, the artery's
A cane, looping down into the belly.
But his aorta's an umbrella
Straining to open: the aneurysm
A furled millefeuille of laminated
Blood, leaked in layers over years,
The arterial walls like batwing skin,
Stretched, distended, between ribs
Of hard fat laid down since childhood.

'This'll keep your hair curly.'
He'd curl up my crusts (always bread
Before cake), '*here, put plenty butter on,*'
A blonde topknot of Lurpak much
Better than marge. I ate them as spirals
Long after I'd left home, outgrown
Curly hair, all his other beliefs.

Backache, we thought, when
He took to his bed. I brought
Food, stayed to talk. He said
Kind, loving things, opened up,
Calm, reflective, as if he knew
Something was finally tearing;
And between us, repairing.

STROKING THE BRAIN

A stroke in the brain starts with an absence
Like a lightning strike, a withdrawal of work.
Something is blocked – an artery, bulging,
Or the blood is escaping somewhere unseen,

Starving some brain cells, whose sugar rush stops.
Each neurone is flagging, depolarising,
Its busy pumping is faltering now.
Potassium is building, instead of leaving,
The cell becomes sick with it, saltier far
Than the sea that surrounds it - water floods in,
In a dangerous swell, a change in the tide.

Until it bursts open, digests itself dying,
Triggering others to fall in their turn,
In radiating rings like dominos falling,
Like silver birches when the meteorite hit Russia,
In forests so dense, it took decades to find.
So like oars stroking, the ripples are spreading,
A tiny tsunami leaving pale, soggy cell skins.
The arteries shut down, til the onslaught is over,
Then pour in hot blood, saving some, failing more.

How to smile, lift a fork, or a foot, how to breathe,
Gone for now, or forever, high and dry on the shore.

LIFTING THE LID
(*Abdominal Aortic Aneurysm*)

Full fathom five in A&E, my father
Lies white as a cuttlefish blade, suddenly granted
The sailor's death war denied him. Water runs
Clear from his mouth and the puncture wounds
Where they pumped in saline to keep his heart afloat
Too late. Holed below the water line, he's drowned,
Awash, beached, bleached, my pale hand red raw beef
Beside his dead man's fingers. Our nails, I see
For the first and last time, are exactly the same shape.
Lividity branches up his sides like coral,
As the corpuscles see-saw and sink,
Silt in the veins. The nurse has battened down
The long-sighted eyes that made him a pilot, too young
For the navy in a war he couldn't wait to join,
After a fisherman's childhood, the curve of cobles
At Cullercoats like the sweep of an eyelid
Over the North Sea's blue.

I think of him sinking, in his sweat-damp bed,
The paramedics baling in vain, his drowning,
Puzzled voice, 'I think I might be dying,'
The aneurysm, an unseen fist in the gut,
An anti-heart, leaking into his belly, blood pressure
Going down, 'I can't breathe,' down, 'can't breathe',
Down for the last time. Swollen as a stranded seal,
As if he'd swallowed the sea, his keel of a chest -
His blanked face - I lift one eyelid, see his eye true blue,
Like those of our Viking ancestors, fierce as the harsh views
He and I fought over, now rinsed clean of blood and rage,
Truly an iris, afloat in its bowl of wet, white china,
Blue as the bruised top of limpet shells
Sanded by tides, the slaty violet of mussels, the white
Like crusts of barnacles, sea-scoured bone.

LAST CALL

Dawn bled out in the sky, as the police drove away,
Leaving me in the street with my aneurysm of news,
So many to tell. Let them sleep, let him live a while
Longer, then I'll let it out, sudden loss of our blood.

My answerphone blinking. His last message, gasping,
His last pain a spear in his side, lancinating,
His agonised voice, 'I'm in a bad way,
You'll have to come down,' and my sleep-stupid
Voice blurting out, 'You mean now?'
I had to erase this last conversation,
Had to pause grief until action was taken,
Certificates issued, his bedding destroyed,
Had to pause it for months, just dribbles escaping,
As grief for my mother still filled every void,
A bulge in my craw that had to burst first.

GHAZAL TO MY LOVER, WHOSE TIME IS NOT ALWAYS MINE.

Your voice on the phone is coconut cream,
But you take so long, my darling;
I wait centuries for your replies,
You take so long, my darling.

I ask a question, but you hesitate,
I hear your thoughts blossom slow as aloes.
Mine are brisk as a North Sea breeze,
But you take so long, my darling.

When I challenge you, make you choose
Between rock and hard place, your silence
Stretches like Caribbean afternoons, because
You take so long, my darling!

So I leap to answer for you, that answer
Makes me angry, so I argue with myself,
While you follow far behind, why
Must you take so long, my darling?

But when we are together, whole days
Pass in your arms, endless slow tides
Of ecstasy, and then, oh then, I love
That you take so long, my darling!

THIS FATAL SUBJECT

Poems of pathology and dissection

A LITTER OF MOONS
(*Foetal specimens, Pathology Museum*)

Brown dwarfs, like Jupiter, we are stars
that didn't make it, too slight to shine.
'Malformed Foetuses': our landfall
broke hearts, though we barely tasted air.
We came in peace, but could not breathe
your atmosphere. Film aliens can be cute:
we dropped into your world to gasps
and screams, at how nature riffs
on your forked symmetry, your skin
with its certainty of inside, outside. Look
at us, how richly we number the ways
cells can combine, or choose to stay apart.

Here a brain balloons, a dark cloud
of thought above the skull. Here, bowels
billow through a split spine. A face
with cartoon eyes slopes straight to cranium
above that comic stare: this has one eye,
a milky navel in mid-brow, where another
has a flaccid horn, a tiny penis bobbing.
Many of us are twin, gazing into identical eyes
across a single body like a seesaw held
in perfect balance, incessant tête à tête.

Tails, fur, tangles of limbs which cannot live
knotted or survive undone: ranged on shelves,
we shine with borrowed light, a litter
of moons. Held suspended, helmeted
in glass, rocked by the footfalls
of those who come to learn from us,
we had a life, though it too was borrowed.
We travelled hopefully, not knowing
until touchdown left us stranded
how you'd fear us, flinch
from our delicate, audacious difference.

SIRENOMELIA BABY

(foetal specimen, pathology museum)

This little mermaid is jarred; feels the moon tug
At the kernel of fluid she floats in. Sealed
So far from the sea, stranded in a tiny glass pool
Beyond the highest tide, she holds hands spread
Like seahorse fins up to her face, as if to scan
A horizon she'll never see. Her eyes are wide,
Avid for distance, for the swell of the ocean's
Breathing, for cold depths to swim in, her sky
A silver skin above. She gasps for salt water.

'Syreniform.' A myth brought to brief life
For a place in seaside freak shows, she floats
As if poured from a genie's lamp. She tapers
From the waist; legs, feet, fused into this blade
Of a tail, no genitals, kidneys, no way out
For the milk she cried for. Born ephemeral
As a damsel fly, this tiddler's a throwback
To a time when we all swam; stranded
By evolution, cut off from our true home.

FROM FIN TO FINGERS

*(programmed cell death, or apoptosis,
in foetal hand formation)*

Our embryo limb buds flower
Into fans, paddles of flesh, as if
Expecting to swim into a tidal rush
Of ocean surging and sighing
Outside the womb's tranquil pool.
But those tides ebbed long ago.
The star-fish rays of bone
That span each human fin
Will need to move in air, grasping,
Waving, fiddling like a lobster's mouth.

And so, the webs between them dissolve
Like a tadpole's tail, as the many cells
Which have held them firm, let go,
Commit cell suicide, no longer hearing
The siren-signal, 'Live!' Nipped in the bud,
Like falling leaves whose end was sealed
By the tree, they slip through our fingers,
Popping like beached sea foam, freeing
Our hands to grow, shaped by the spaces
Carved out in utero, from fin to fingers.

'GIRL HAS SECOND HEAD REMOVED'
(Headline: Craniopagus Parasiticus,
Egypt, 2005, 2006)

It's the splitting and the parting: it's hard
To let go. We clung three days too long,
So our crowns touched, and took, grafted
And grew. My blood dried like unwanted
Milk, so she suckled me through our skulls,
My twin, myself, our two brains
Sharing one swollen cartouche of bone.
Our faces are the same, but below mine
Is a mere knob of bone and skin. So
She is the baby girl, I am 'the parasite',
'It', an affliction she struggles to feed, for
She is my heart, and her heart falters often.
Only one nurse has named me. I watch them,
Kind eyes below turned-down smiles,
Tending, cradling her, my dead weight
Tagged on, unwanted. My presence
Is a wonder of the world, yet I am
The absence of a child, offered
Empty bottles, my blinking, suckling,
Noted as 'reflexive signs.' I've never
Breathed air, or tasted milk. I cry in silence,
My face, tongue, working in protest;
No lungs, no consciousness, they think.

When they chose to divide us, the men
Of medicine and religion, they cut
Me off like a wart, harvesting my skull
For patching hers, leaving us both
Diminished, as her brain swelled, beating
Itself against bone, as if seeking mine.

Like our nation's conjoined faiths,
We could never quite part, or live like sisters.
She ceased to smile once I had ceased to cry:
She gave me life, I showed her how to die.

CYCLOPS BABY
(foetal specimen)

We are divided creatures, reflecting
Ourselves in a midline mirror; right
And left define us. Antagonistic,
Adversarial, always taking sides.
And so the brain must split
Into hemispheres, the face forming
Like chrysanthemum petals curling
To touch, to merge, to place
Two eyes, nose, mouth,
Universal emoticon.

Not this time. This hefty infant is not
In two minds. Her brain is one,
The mirror of her face distorted,
And so she's Cyclops, this strapping
Baby girl with perfect limbs,
With one big central eye a navel
In her face, the pupil transverse
Like a squid's, and above it,
A tiny trunk, a proboscis
Of wrinkled skin hanging.

Her undivided brain did not survive
Once born, but was there some
Awareness, did she feel light,
Briefly, perhaps as a plant does?
Lambs, kids, born with Cyclops
Eye, were the model for the myth:
False Hellebore eaten in pregnancy,
Or muddled genes, that's all it takes
To make a single mind and eye, blight
The petals of the flowering face.

BENIGN

Portrait by Lam Qua of Kwan Meiurh, before surgery by
Dr Peter Parker, 1838. Surgery had been forbidden in China by
Confucianism. (Gordon Museum of Pathology, London)

A peeled wand of a woman, she has opened her robe
For Lam Qua. The tumour her left breast has become
Hangs like a wasp's nest, humming hot with blood, big
As a pregnant belly she must carry like a child, her arm
Gingerly hefting its tender weight. Pink milk
Seeps from the raw gland, red as the carp she paints
With silk, each strand split forty, fifty times. She knows
About slow growing, her embroidery coming into focus
Hair by invisible hair, in the long months her breast fed itself
To this fruition; her blind, dependent twin, its pulse
The measure of her labouring heart.

She is calm,
Watching Qua's brush, brutal, swift like the knife
Of the ghost-white foreigner he paints for. Tomorrow,
She will lie down for Dr Parker, welcoming the pang
Of separation, her face impassive as his steel dissects
Her conscious flesh. Given as a gift, his alien skill
He hopes will win her for his god
Of whom there are no pictures, will right her
To live on, obscure and tranquil, her painted face gazing
On our land of ghosts, who flinch from the ripe, doomed
Adenoma seething below her fine-drawn, patient stare.

SAUSAGES AFTER AMPUTATION

(portrait by Lam Qua before surgery of Leang Yen, with
osteo-medullary sarcoma of right hand and wrist, 1838.)

Oily sausages. Fat, mottled, glistening, they steam
In my mind's mouth, as Dr Parker saws through the meat
Of my right arm, and into the bone. Forced into the skin
Of my wrist, the tumour makes blood pudding of my hand,
A fungoid lump, from which the cockscomb of my fingers
Waggles. Ah, this disease has gobbled me up. How long
Will my husband stay with a wife that shames him?
Why does Parker, with his white man's blade, want
My monstrous wrist? Why would he work for nothing? So
I asked *him* for money, you should have seen his face!
I'm supposed to be grateful, you see, swallow his religion.
But this is Canton, everything is for sale.

Oily sausages. Fat fingers overstuffed with meat, sizzling
In my head as the saw bites. My mouth waters.
They gave me opiates, while outside,
An opium dealer's execution ends in riot.
I hear the crowd's puzzled resentment, like mine,
When I knew my arm was forfeit. Lam Qua painted
My slim left arm, my swollen right, my shrouded face.

My arm has gone, a gift for Parker's greedy god,
They are sewing the flap of skin, and all I can think of
Are oily sausages. I shall devour them,
Gorge on them, with no rice, only the meat.

IN THE DISSECTING ROOM.

The boy slices an old man's scrotum, his face
Intent, inches above the pouch and the thick hump
Of penis. A girl scrapes at the abdomen of a woman
Of ninety, the turned-back skin flap
Backed with creamy fat like wet sheepskin.
But though lying naked on steel drainage tables,
These are not victims. These are not
The tabloids' 'frail pensioners'. Veterans
Of the war on gravity, they are massive, grand,
Muscular, with beautiful strong necks, chins
Superbly jutting, hefty thighs and calves. The genitals
Seen from this angle are surprisingly big, roomy,
Solid and durable, unselfconsciously exposed.

The faces we can see are grave, unwrinkled,
Filled out by death and formalin. Some
Are veiled by cauls of sacking, the students
Avoiding their silent teachers' eyes.
Clutches of gorgeous boys and girls glow
Amber, rose and gold, clustering round
The ivory dead, like exotic birds pecking
Nervously at the skin of splendidly indifferent
Rhinos. The bloodless bodies display
Something few of the living attain:
The ability to simply be, without apology
For imperfection, without awareness of
How they look. This is what gives them
Their final outward beauty, as the scalpels
Scrape, exposing the beauty within
Which has been there all the time.

DISSECTION SUITE: TEN OBLIQUE VIEWS

I

Teeth grin in the dead mouths. Small, neat, stained.
Here, a row missing, the lower lip sucked into the hole
Of the collapsed mouth, chin bristles alert, going over the top
Into the dark gape, like prickles of music on a pianola roll.

II

Hands lie curled, white fingers plump
With liquid, knuckles pressed flat
By handling and hard storage, all resilience
Lost. This old woman, face lined, hands
Mauve, has shiny, immaculate nails,
Long and manicured, showing no sign
Of how many dresses in shops, how many
Lovers, how many children's chubby legs
Her hands stroked, of when they struck,
Gave, touched, defended, put to rights.

III

Joined at the hip by genitals, a pair of thighs
Lie on a table, the sawn-off ends each showing
A button of bone, small discs of femur, offset
In an oval of muscle and fat. The skin has pursed itself
Around the amputations, as if trying to heal.

A head in a steel bowl looks through parted legs.

IV

Nipple left standing
On the lung; breast skin turned back,
A round hole in it.

V

X-ray on the lit screen:
'Barium swallow.'
A St Christopher medal hangs
Askew, as if swinging, a clear-cut
Silver pendulum, rising on the curve
Of the ghostly breast, its shadow
A bowed head impaled on the oesophagus.

VI

Shaved heads, breasts flattened
Empty pouches; with genitals covered,
Difference of sex no more we show;
No more than different races do.

VII

Breastbones in a box
Like stingless white scorpions:
Scuttling cuttlebones.

VIII

Disembodied faces efface themselves, so small,
So flimsy, so exposed. Peeled from their skulls,
They regain expression, become wry, humorous, wise:
One with windpipe attached, a deflated balloon on a string.

IX

Bloodless, the flesh
Shows its true colours
Like autumn leaves drained
Of green – apricot, peach,
Taupe, beige, mushroom,
Cream, shell pink, yellow.

X

'Cause of death' cut down to size
By its own acronym – COD PARKINSONS,
COD GASTRIC CARCINOMA, COD LUNG CANCER.

'INDEFINITE RETENTION'

Skeletons flaunt jaunty cranium skull caps,
Flat sliced faces squaring up to an afterlife
Of suspension. Heavy handed, their arms
Hang behind the twin Africas
Of their pelvic blades, unlike ours
Which are always in front of us.

This one twists its head away, ribcage cartilage
Blackened, as if from standing too near the fire.
I lift one slender foot, finger the elegant blunt spur
Of the os calcis, navicular, cuboid, following
In the intact umber bones the tracks of the impact,
Its faultlines still crackling through my feet.

SLICES OF BRAIN.

Third anniversary of my mother's death from dementia,
And I'm looking at slices of brain, stained pretty pink,
The neurones purplish, their nuclei clear as strawberry pips.

Like a magician in his many-coloured coat of patches, motley
Bow tie, hair like wild dendrites in a frenzy of thinking,
The pathologist initiates me into what death has revealed.

The donor's name is on the slides, their memorial, evidence
Of how memory escaped them. Alzheimer and his mates
(Lewy Body, Parkinson, Vascular, alone or in cahoots)

Miss no tricks. Tau Proteins strangle and swamp, cutting off
The synapses, keeping the thoughts corralled in tangles,
Scribbles of barbed wire around the nucleus, sometimes

Killing the cell like a rubber band round a lamb's balls,
So a ghost tangle is left, guarding empty space.
(Are there ghost memories inside?) Ameloid proteins

Lag the axons, the dendrites, the outreaching fronds
Which pass torches of thought, until
There's a plaque, like a fingertip print

Stubbed on the connections. Scattered booby traps,
You have to look out for them. Cortical, hippocampal
Layers, like lagoons and sandy beaches, slide after slide,

Pebbled with tangles, wracked with plaques,
In a shrinking brain losing weight and substance,
Because there's 'vacuolation', holes where words were.

And it happens, we don't feel it, until it's noticed by our friends,
And called a senior moment, until there are too many moments
To be funny any more.

RAT BRAIN:
WAVING NOT DROWNING

Delta, theta, alpha, beta, gamma:
This sliver of rat brain, suspended
In a beaker of bubbling broth, still
Emits waves, its neurones firing,
Recharging, firing, for hours, even
Days. It's hard to believe I'm not
Watching it thinking; the oscillations
Printing out like ranges of crazy hills
Could be peaks of squeaks, twitches
Of chopped off tail or whisker, thoughts
Of sex or scraps, circling like rats
In a cage, with no way out. Even
Governments have their doubts, even
A lab rat might still think, worse, know
It's still thinking, with a whole brain:
Too horrible to allow, even to scientists
Who breed, euthanize, dissect. Hence
This mere shaving of hippocampus,
Firing away at nothing. How aware
Of itself would your brain be, alive
In a sensory deprivation tank? Thinking
About consciousness with our conscious
Mind is hard. Harder, to imagine
Its absence, using the same unvarying,
Inescapable equipment, chasing our
Mental tails round the cages of our skulls.

Delta, theta, alpha, beta, gamma: each
Tide of waves newly detected, washes us closer
To what we don't yet know, what other
Electrical storms crackle, waving
Bravely, unseen; may be waving now,
In this submerged slice of rat, signalling
Mayday, mayday, in rodent morse.

FACE RAT
(Human Pathology Specimen, London)

For years, it gnawed away her face,
Room 101's worst nightmare; not hers.
Hers must have been to lose it, the rat,
The rodent ulcer, which slowly ate
Her nose, brow, cheekbone, eye.
Wispy-haired, her head floats in its jar,
A large slice shockingly cut out. The way
She must have looked when found
By the brother who fed his reclusive
Sister for years, unseen until
The day the food stayed on the step.
The tragedy, they said, was that she hid
Her deformity away, ashamed, when
Early caught, the cancer can be clean cut off.

But meeting her pale eye, I wonder. From a wart
That scabbed, never healed, to *this*: she had time
To choose, before so much was lost, to lose
The ulcer. Unless she chose to keep it, feed it,
Feel it nibbling through the night like a pet
Licking her face, something to love, and give
Herself to. The tragedy was, perhaps, it died
When she did; the blessing, she was not alone.

HANDYMAN
(pathologist's death scene photograph)

His young face on the pillow is dark, serene,
Handsome, gazing up at the guillotine
Which cut off his head, straddling his bed
Like an open doorway. Better with tools
Than people; his father's disappointment
A snag he couldn't sand smooth. Silence
Was a fuse melting, hot-wired between them.

But *'What's he up to in there? Using the electric,
Running up bills...'* drilled
Into his skull through the wall
As he hammered, sawed, planed, his wood, metal, stone.

He chose to look up: to see that it worked, or
To welcome its coming, hot through his throat?
When he thrust with the stick, that switched on the saw,
That cut through the rope, that let fall the blade,
That cut off his head, serene on the pillow – how long
A head lives, how long its eyes see, is something he knew
That we don't, and whether, how long, it hurt less than living.

And as the blade fell, it released the rod, that switched off
The saw, that cut off his father's complaint, when
He found him, about *'using the electric, and running up bills'*.

FIGHTING FIRE

'A characteristic of burned bodies is their...
'pugilistic attitude''. Gaute & Odell.

We are all firefighters, heroes
Waiting for the big match, ready
To take on the undefeatable, the hot
Favourite.

    Roaring out of its corner,
It engulfs us in its bear hug, squeezes
The breath from us, claws the flesh
From our bones, eats the light from us,
Wins.

    Fallen, we fight on, snarling
At death like bodies at Pompeii, fists
Raised in pugilistic attitude, stripped
And bare knuckled, fired into permanent
defiance.

POEMS OF EVOLUTION
AND AFRICA

IN THE BEGINNING WAS THE BANG

So this was the start of it, a tiny dot
In empty space. Except it had no size,
And it was nowhere, as all space
Was inside it, with time, and light,
And polo mints, neutrinos, socialism
And Britney Spears, until it burst,
Creating its own start time. It's bursting
Now, flinging splatters of gas and galaxies
Into the space it makes, like
Local Authorities throw up houses
Where playing fields aren't.

So we celebrate it today, with lots
Of little bangs, flinging splatters
Of human material into the space
Where towns and trees were, casting
Nebulae of dust into the sky
Like the clouds that gave birth to stars.
But our sparks go out, while space goes on
Running away from us, always escaping.

CRUNCHING THE NUMBERS

Millions of billions of years: three
Generations of stars bloomed and burst,
Flinging their heavy seeds
Into the tilth that became Earth.

Billions more years
Preparing the ground: sun, water,
Air, mixed just right, until life
Germinated.

Millions more years
From cell, to fish, to frog,
To lizard, to mouse,
Dodging the dinosaurs,
And the disaster that killed them.

Thousands more years
To become aware we are
Human, the few survivors
Of numberless chances,
Coincidences, mutations.

All but five of every hundred
Of us conceived still die
Unborn. So we here, now,
Children of the fittest of the fit,
Are the winners. But contemplating
Death, our own, is it any wonder
We feel it can't, just can't
Be the end, there must be more?

SONIC THE HEDGEHOG KILLED YOUR BABY
A sonnet.

What we create, is ours to give a name:
What we discover, we feel we have created.
Thus the designers of computer games:
Thus two geneticists. They anticipated
Renown, respect of peers, a Nobel prize;
While playing wanton gods with lab fruit flies,
They identified a gene, which when awry,
Raised spiny bumps upon an embryo fly.
Gung ho with pride, their alpha-minds decided
To name 'their' gene for the hedgehog from Japan.
 But not so cute, that same flaw coincided
In human babies, resulting in a scan
Revealing Cyclops eye, a malformed brain,
Disability, early death. To fathers and mothers
It jars to hear the culprit's frivolous name;
A prize for some, heartbreak and havoc for others.

Not meant of course, but it could have been expected:
Genetics tells us, all life is connected.

DARK MATTERS
(substantia nigra, the melanin inside the brain)

Inside, all our brains are black. I've seen it, fossil traces
Of how we all looked, when melanin shaded us
From the burn and blight of African sun. Those born
Pale sickened, became nobody's ancestors. We children
Of those who thrived, still carry a coaly seam of it
In our heads, our minds growing blacker as we grow wiser:
A by-product of thinking, like art, and war, and dreaming,
Til it dwindles with dementia, fading with memory. So
Let us celebrate neuromelanin, the dark matter
Within the grey, the white, the red. Let us celebrate
Melanocytes, for flipping up tiny black parasols to
Keep the stark sun's harm from our cells; and for
Learning to keep them furled by random mutation
As some of us moved north, lest our bones crumble
Through lack of light. Now we can choose
Where we live, wear clothes, hats, SPF50, make fire,
Take vitamin D, our skins still show how evolution
Cared for us until we learned to care for ourselves,
If not yet, sufficiently for one another.

WALKING BACK TO AFRICA

The desert, seen from high above, is scrawled
With the wind's mysterious graffiti. I try to read
These hieroglyphs: wavy lines, claw marks, a group
Of neat horseshoes like sheepfolds. Even a cluster
Of houses, far out in the middle of this nowhere,
Perched on the stem of a thin road which ends
At their heart, must mean something, if only
I knew the code. But it's Africa, below me,
Rising to meet me, and part of me is coming home.

As the plane flies, I am walking, walking back
To Africa, past my mother in her fifties frocks,
And my grandmother in her twenties shoes,
And her mother with her shawl and solid strength,
Past all their mothers, from the cold north east of England
Back to Africa, and my original, many times great,
Many times grand, mother. While the wheels kiss
The runway, while I wheel my case along lines as straight
As desert roads, I am walking back to her, though she
Will not know me, and by the time I am reading my name
On a placard held by a man sent to drive me, I have reached
Her. Five hours to fly, just one hour to walk
Across oceans, continents, generations, bridge
Hundreds of thousands of years of evolution and adventure.

COMING TO EGYPT TO WRITE ABOUT DEATH

My lungs and lights were sealed in a canopic jar
Of ice. Egyptian sun has splintered it, as in England
Blackbirds are chip, chip, chipping away at winter
With their new-coined beaks.
Now, marinaded in the swimming pool's blue
Natron, sunbaked dry of northern phlegm, I lie
In a high vaulted room of marble and tile,
My retainer protruding from my lips like
Tutankhamen's teeth, arms at my sides, thinking
Of death and pathology. My laptop makes settling
Noises, like a fire that's baked its own crust,
Or the hot bright walls of this kiln of a house,
A canopic jar of fire and earth. Mosquitoes
Lie dead, their questioning bodies dry as tiny dunes,
Sacrificed to my rest by wafts of unguents.

Here my heart will be weighed, and found lighter.

ON BEING SEXUALLY AROUSED BY THE CHEVIOT HILLS

Turning onto the top road, across the winter fields I glimpse
Cheviot, its long bone highlighted in snow, and I feel it,
That sweet sudden ache in my groin, like the hard hot buzz
In my jeans pocket, where his texts reach me before his words.
Now Cheviot is texting me, its swollen curve of finger
Calling me awake, so driving past I judder, hot in my seat.

No obscure fetish this, though, but a chat-up line. Mine.
Exchanging emails, flirting our way from friendship
Into frantic fling, I told him, 'I can see Cheviot from my bed,'
The invitation there, unsaid. Successful, too.
And it was true, I could then, when the trees stood stiff
But five years shorter in Sainsbury's car park, winter-bare.
Now I see it from my car, and he still drives three hundred miles
To make me come, and come, rising and falling like the Cheviots,
Where curlews warble like a ringtone in the tight denim slot
Across the curve of my thigh. That's why now, desire burns
Like a gorse fire, blossoming at the sight of a modest mountain.